ANITA GOVAN was born in Stirling and lives in Edinburgh, where she has been actively involved in the artistic community for over sixteen years. Although she was discovered to be severely dyslexic at the age of ten, her creative delight in the possibilites of language remains irrepressibly dynamic. She trained as a professional ballet dancer until the tragic death of her mother when she was seventeen. From 2001 to 2004 she co-produced Big Word, inaugurating the first performance poetry slams in Scotland and organising regular performance poetry events around the country. A passionate advocate of poetry, she runs workshops in communities and schools and has performed in various countries, including Ireland, the United States and the Czech Republic. Further information can be found at www.anitagovan.com.

Jane

ANITA GOVAN

Luath Press Limited

EDINBURGH

www.luath.co.uk

KIRKLEES METROPOLITAN COUNCIL	
250603333	
Bertrams	24.10.06
821.92	£6.99
HU	CUL42620

First published 2005

The paper used in this book is recyclable.
It is made from low-chlorine pulps produced in a low-energy,
low-emission manner from renewable forests.

The publisher acknowledges subsidy from the Scottish Arts Council

Scottish
Arts Council

towards the publication of this volume.

Printed and bound by
DigiSource GB Ltd, Livingston

Typeset in 11 point Sabon

To Winifred Lennox Govan & Ian Grant Govan, my parents, who gave me their love and faith, which sustains me always.

Acknowledgements

Thanks to all my friends and family, especially Patricia Muñoz for her dedication, advice and artistic dialogue; to my children, Shaun, Zoe and Callum for their love and understanding; to Lara McDonald for all her support and to Jennie Renton for her encouragement, and help with my Dragon. I am indebted to everyone who has inspired me over the years, particularly Margaret Doran, the primary school teacher who nourished my love of language. I am grateful to the Scottish Arts Council and everyone at Luath Press.

Contents

Light

they that know
the truth of it
with such brilliant colour
in bright-eyed remembrance
its breath upon the fire
a light
that feeds
the very birth of it
shattering
into the quiet chaos
like some bright bell
in still silence
a moment
to change the world

Three monkeys and me

three monkeys three monkeys three monkeys and me
sitting, sitting, sitting in a monkey-puzzle tree

one cannot see

blinded, blinded by all those things
he collected near and dear
shiny trinkets that he gathered like a king
piling them high, high up against his fear
up against that phantom thief that might appear
guarding his 'precious' that ball and chain
muttering the bitter injustice of his fate
for he's the prisoner behind his fortress walls
yet his empty eyes speak of hunger still
that greedy knot he cannot will not fill

three monkeys three monkeys three monkeys and me
sitting, sitting, sitting in a monkey-puzzle tree

one cannot hear

his voice so very, very loud
he drowns us all within its stony sound
he rants and raves of all us evil-doers
he a righteous man amongst all us sinners
with parrot words he spits his anger
listening to nothing that does not mirror
the narrow path of his written text
a book of truths he has swallowed whole

that concrete wisdom he has gathered in his quest
a soapbox clown with lava words of hate and death

three monkeys three monkeys three monkeys and me
sitting, sitting, sitting in a monkey-puzzle tree

one cannot speak

he sits in dark silence
glued to a silvery screen
popping his pills and snorting his dreams
as his buzzing thoughts just steam, steam
with all the injustice his eyes have seen
yet he forgot long ago how to utter 'NO'
but still he struggles now and then
caught in the straightjacket of his own aching head
till his last and thawing thoughts
just trickle down his chin

three monkeys three monkeys three monkeys and me
sitting, sitting, sitting in a monkey-puzzle tree

and then there's me

I am just a small bird
sitting in a tree
looking at all the beauty
the world can offer me

but Oh
Oh how I weep

I weep for thee
you silly mad
mad monkey three

for you cannot speak
nor hear
nor even see

the mess you've made
the mess you've made

here in the monkey-puzzle tree

Reality's love bites

did I
but dream this thing

then
let me awake
to sleep again
within its arms

I
the constant dreamer
catching paradise

here
my heaven dwells

Sky-loch

we talked
weighted by the burdens of the daily
this moment
rimmed with silver
across the car-park
cracked tarmac
crumbling and half empty

in this stumbling
snapshot
we stopped
caught
within a still and frozen sea breath
its astonished magic
a nameless dew-drop
fixing our wandering eyes
as its blue isle
cleared
those bright shores
caught within its halting sky

lost and hooked like silver fishes
we stood
caught together
within the crook
of childhood eyes
watching
in concrete silence
the cast away wishes

the idle Pooh sticks
driftwood
between its tumbleweed clouds

smiling with wonder
we both sighed
cast off and glowing
from its suspended glory
an understanding settling within our eyes
no word spoken
just this fleeting treasure
here beneath its sky-loch skies

ambling we talked
across the car park
cracked tarmac
crumbling and half empty

this moment rimmed with silver
imprinted
forever
in my mind's eye

Buba-Jane's mother

to remember her

a piece of good furniture
matured oak
giving a subtle smile
to the bits of tittle-tattle
that make their way into
her easy ear

to think of her

the world spinning – an axis
her shoulder heaving heavy with its time
that knock
of absent thought
to think what could have been

to look at her

a tatty unseen shadow
ragged at the edges
that gives the room an air of passing
that lived-in feeling
loved by all and then forgotten
for those better distant dreams

to know her

a woman of the infinite
a guru of the world
that way of being

Your eyes

to seek the beautiful
the blue
between sea and shore
lost grains of time
dull chimes
in child's play

the drunken heathered skies
rumbling
with roaring purple
spitting
in mercury rain

as the shadows stumble
and the light begins to fade

here the 'still'
remains

sediments of a million pasts
lying unbroken
in breathless wait
with sucking seeds
bright-flush stars
beneath our stony way

beneath this cradle
beneath this grave
the beauty
between
each brief and passing day

Black butterfly

picture this
picture this

dawn's dusty veil
painting gray
the dampened tar streets
salty spray
brisk winds that nip
at the tips
of frosty fingers
a cool arousal
a stiff slap
full in your face

raw and rare
raw and rare
this crack
this crack
this crack of bitter air

notice him there
notice him
still and sitting
the Buddha of littered streets
half empty
his hat cast before him
blue-lipped and stuttering
a misplaced mantra
crammed up

pinned in a doorway
this black butterfly
caught quivering
on a grey slab
butchered
his fate
just spinning
spinning
spinning in the restless wind
sitting on the edge

two worlds
just looking in
looking in
looking in
at all those shiny things

he hailed me
I tossed some change
lit his fag
his city-black hands
clutching
his only comfort
a doe-eyed dog
a patchwork angel
sitting at the feet of God
curled up and sleeping
in a sea of strangers
this bright pearl to his love
reflected in a fragile smile

I
blinded by time
pushing
pushing against its brim
glanced back briefly
to see his fragile smile
washed away in a sea of empty faces
gobbled up in these tangled streets of plenty
where cars trundle
in lazy ease
their sealed-in treasures
locked tight
tight
tight behind

smoky veils
smoky veils

of glass tinted roses

Awake

a switch clicks
vacant dreams slip by
vanish upon an urgent cry
a scream

you heave
your drugged and dragging feet
a body in rebellious wake
down the hall to greet a face in pain

suckled now
silent now
relief mixed-in
reluctant anger
slumber at war
with consciousness

this wrecked ship
stands with haunted hulk
echoing the hollow sound
of a lost lullaby
a lullaby
cast into silence now

in silence now
a whispering breath
dips
rises
falls

beyond these shores

while you stand
the guardian
of another's dreams

Here I

so many times
hidden
silent
between the gaps
the unseen
where to live
is a constant journey of moments
pushed-back curtains
to peek
to steal
out into a world that watches
every flicker
every moan
from the creaking boards
where the actor plays
magician
of tantalising dreams

hidden I

behind this curtain
veiled from gaze
a masquerade
of reinvention
quickly forgotten
pre-stage jitters
hidden
fraying collar
loose button

fading lipstick
the lick
of fear
a terror of being
stripped naked
to devouring eyes
that watch
in anticipation

neither I

the watcher-magician
here a comma
a full stop
onlooker of hidden realities
the lost and longing
stumbling to make sense of chaos
knowing
but fragmented jigsaw moments
a constant longing to rip
to shred this mask
this empty shell
of emperor's clothing

here I

the invisible link
who bathes
engulfed in shadows of silence
burnt by fires
of internal dreams

Mother's Day

why don't you give the devil a bunch of flowers
she's the fallen angel cast from her tower
a paradise lost where that first love was born
deep within your breast
those fresh lips which stuttered her name
devoured her whole frame

for your own sake she left you
weeping
greeting
writhing in pain
on a pyre of your own making

Goddess
Witch
Madonna
Whore
she the devil
'your secret desire'
why don't you give her a bunch of flowers

Pebbles

all these things I tried to say
falling as
bleached bones
shattered at the ends of days

all these rich hopes
escaped
fragile with neglect
misty moments blown away

all these things
forgot
fragments lost
washed smooth and round

just pebbles
now

one skipped thrice across the loch
before it drowned

Unborn

I'll miss the skip
that beat
that frees my lips to kiss

I'll miss the yawning gap
the silence
between sleep upon the verge of morning's lap

I'll miss this song that sings
within the midst
a chaotic muse of bliss

I'll miss the wild-eyed
morning stare
crawling from my hovelled lair

I'll miss the wind that sweeps
horizons
beyond the seas

I'll miss the good looks of Eve
as she weaves her trailing feet
that lead to my final peace

I'll miss all this
and more
the things that I have never seen

Ah! but to live was my greatest dream

Ariel

let us sit
let us sit and watch
where once I was caught
out in those twisting webs
the frosty doubts
a demon child in a winter sea-storm

above the tempest
your faint notes found me
those plucking strings
the lost chords a perfect fit
a compass of laughter
a sparkling sea-road I could not resist
a numb child adrift
in a warm sea-spring flow
thawing
thawing in its gentle glow

I found this your resting place
chance full of sunny embrace
castaways gazing
between star-pearled eyes
watching the coloured sunrise
jamming our pockets
with its sandy grains
stolen moments from Prospero's gaze

and yet this isle is but a dream
this keeping comfort

in which I sleep and sing
these your seagull wings
catching each morning
on the changing air
the lapping beats
those scented sea notes
cutting free
your earthly moorings
those many binding strings

and when you leave
caught upon that unexpected wind
I shall sleep
nestling long within those echoed beats
that ring of pearly laughter
this note to follow on
a different story
in the here and ever after

The devil

the devil rides upon her back
chanting
screaming
that greedy wind
scratching worry in her eyes

she bends she bows
the whims of her peers
the countless eyes
condemn her life
tear her limb from limb
dare she raise her voice against the din

she YELLS
an Amazon possessed
reeling from that moralistic hum
that sharp knife-edge
collides with its dark shroud
beneath her breast
a victim
of ritualistic slaughter
consumed
devoured
fallen now
and yet

a goddess on her last breath
she sighs to see
the eye of heaven above

Born

a newborn blush
with haphazard care
tossed
with ripe and ripping lungs
screams
with glorious melody
a soft and smelling being
suckled with hope
triumphant
in life's ear
joins now this chorused hum here

and at the moment of vital spark
now joined in fresh voice
that first bite of life is grasped
stumbling
wide-eyed upon its path
to that perpetual drum
internal dance
which the empress
alone commands

a newborn blush
with haphazard care
tossed
with ripe and ripping lungs
screams
with glorious melody
with glorious melody

Kitchen

she slips from
space to space
swaying shifting
baby hung on hip
like a stone
a stone
to and fro
to and fro
stirring that hot pot
as child sits
on wide hip
rhythms of her body sing

a quick step
from counter
to cooker
to fridge
the table now set
gleaming
as the radio natters and chatters

now she
in that moment
stands still at sink
vacant
while sounds of a distant jungle ring

These words

these words
these words are naked
stripped bare to the bone
an inch from the edge of this endless road
fiery bright shots
straight and clear
straight, straight into
the living atmosphere

these words
these words are my dreams
a cherry ripe seed bomb
of daisy diamond ideas
a revolution
hatched
with a butterfly kiss
a brainteasing bloomer
jamming up the air waves

these words
these words are my flesh my blood
my body their vessel
a golden cup
of dambusting passion
an ocean of thirst
that rushes as rivers
to quench this dusty earth

these words
these words are my rage
the protest from my page
the hungry forgotten
the new wageslave
struggling each morning
trying to pass
through each ghostly day

these words
these words are my sword
my bid to find freedom
in my top drawer
my feint
my parry
my peace of mind
to wake in the morning
without fear in my mind

these words
these words are my prayers
shiny bright faces
caught unawares
the untarnished dreamers
who never despair
and sparkle like glitter
just to be here

these words
these words are my shooting stars
a constellation of thoughts

that fell from the skies
those faint grains of hope
that brought
tears to my eyes

these words
these words are my universe
the future
the past
the echoes of ages
embedded with blood
the many who have fallen
and planted their love

these words
these words are my art
my god
a thousand thoughts that stumble and flow
an inch from the edge
of this endless road
an inch from the edge
of this endless road

Hero

a hero has few words

and so he laid a white sheet
blue-veined and quiet
his soft skin cold to touch
such a precious thing
his life
tucked up in linen
and queuing for death
his shallow breath a shadow

I was blessed to know him

keeping his light close
at night
a child in secret
creeping to check his heart
still beat beneath the sheets
at peace my hero
invincible
the world turned back to right

here in time's erosion

we sat handholding
my foolish thoughts
dissipating into deep silence
the parting at journey's end
a rich tapestry woven

into each crease each fold
the last stitches
knotted and cut with care

where a hero has few words
and only time fills the void

Mandela's garden

he emerged a symbol
threaded silver hair
walrus wrinkled
a blueprint still
hidden behind a smile
through all his woes
his patience
of that long road
ending at a rusty gate

here into a glaring world
he stepped
its flashing fangs
gobbling up
the first of him
the last of him
his offering
now presented
for the payment of his dream

watching TV
I stopped arrested
sipping my hot tea
a wayward tear
unchecked
down my cheek
I longed to shake his hand
thank him
hoped he would

for a time
find his peace
his garden
peopled with a thousand seeds
watch them grow
walk with freedom
around each petalled flower
rest untarnished
in its golden hour

far away
far away
from this glaring beast

and me

Cherry blossom dreams

I often watch in flashes
hammock hung
beneath its chest
cradled in its boughs
of autumn rest
flickering memories
the first bloom of glory
I a child in dormant spring
buried in blossom
the joys of life
giggling under the dome
a crisp clear sky
held high
beyond the touch
of death

Mirror

bury me deep
beneath the blossom
and do not weep
this tomb
this bower
is but for dusty bones
a veil
now fallen

but seek
a ripe reflection
hope grown strong
from seed to tree
with open hearts
and threads of love
look again
for me

Unpicked fruit

cramming
cramming this idle time with trinkets
absent remembrances
unpicked passions that linger still
with bated breath
a serpent's whisper laying its purple thirst
upon a restless river
filling to its brim
casting up its casual treasures
those star-scattered wishes
that glittered
then slipped with ease from the fingers of youth
unnoticed
untouched specks of dew
melting into that misty dim
those many fallen fruits
that twinkle with a mocking grin

here Eve and I wander together
gathering its harvest upon its banks
the sisters of sin in our idle imaginings
dipping our toes our fingertips
tracing at its dark edge its watery skin
sucking upon its rim
the drops of time from Neptune's table
those many mirrored island pools
broken reflections
pasts and presents
that glimmer with a shuttered blink

Ah, this fool's gold
and all the futures
that quickly dwindle to nothing
nothing
on parched and thirsty lips

with broken tongues we sing
we sing its song of silence
mermaids stranded
drowning with Ophelia's madness
sitting with the tattered angels
cracked and cramming their stony jars
the fruited remnants the shattered remains
all the burdens of what might once have been

beneath these empty branches we sit
cradling ripe thoughts in vacant pockets
spying the unexpected
seeds of regret
that brief and familiar silhouette
that snatches
catches at the breath
in this lullaby of quiet decay

till at last an earthworm's pierce
consumes its fallen prey
picks clean its empty chamber
this forgotten carcass
marked unknown and missing

Dr Love

it's a funny thing
a funny thing
that creeps inside your skin
just the little things
the easy pregnant pauses
where the breath is golden strings
and its gentle notes fall softly
into the break of every conversation

it's such a funny thing
such a funny thing
a cat that jumps on springs
and leaps with joys unbound
into every vein
and cannot settle down
until it scratches all its doubts
into those chance upon a time
meetings

Oh it's such a funny thing
such a funny thing
that rings and sings
inside your head
the echo of each and
every moment
which is then
rewound
rewound again
from the slightest touch

that tingles in your guts
to a strange and knowing frown
that sends you in a rush
chasing racing
into new
and unexpected ground

Oh what is this thing
this silly thing
that ties you up in knots
and fiddles with your head
until at last you're caught
entangled in its web
with all those sticky thoughts
that drive you round the bend

and now of course
you'll never sleep
in a still and empty bed

Oh save me
save me
save me please
from this funny thing

the sting
of Dr Love

Love

I mistook you for an angel by the door
fresh-faced in your crumpled dark suit
that open white linen smile
freshly ironed
cupid with choir boy eyes
boasting a touch of infectious immortality

loitering between scheme queens and bullyboy doormen
rock chicks screamed to you on cluttered pavements
throwing up their hearts
beating on their chests
how you left them high and dry
and how they'll never love again

a sharking king in moon's full-blooded blossom
we met to monster wrestle to the last
and I as Icarus fell
your conversation voice rich in timbre steps
till the last dram was drained
and the empty streets left
littered
in the carnage of your perfumed wake

Bar stool angels

she arrived in peppered heels
tapping in Morse code
the notes of a blind man's tune
on marble floors
platinum-bottled hair
rock-sprayed
neatly swaying through the smoky air
crisscrossing the bar-room chatter
fuschia-lipped in cocktail pink
her perfume exhaling a long breath

keeping company with ghosts she hummed a bird
perfecting the art of imprinting lipstick to glass
caught in the tilt of private conversations
nailing each cigarette into the blossom

bare and fragile she sat upon a thread

Sleeping in the arms of slumber

sleeping in the arms of slumber
I awoke in a bed of cinders
white heather
stained purple
the voice of Agamemnon
whispers

awake...awake
the deed is done
the deed is done
the kiss has come

beneath the rubble
amnesia

many lay still
white-faced and silent
suffocated
in the choke of dark
home and hearth
broken murmurs
of a death chant

the deed is done
the kiss has come
the kiss has come

fragments of a lady's mirror
lay shattered

blinking with a million eyes
as a magpie stumbles
with its stolen treasures
brave thoughts and deeds
the bloodied toils of
hands and feet
all shredded in the slow

tick
tick
tick

the kiss has come
the kiss has come

awake...awake

D's for Dragons

D's for Dragons
D's for Dragons
D's for Dragons
the teacher said

it staked me out
staked my every move from birth
weaving its smoky breath
in and out
in and out
curling its tongue
a multicoloured spiral
above my bed
fanning its embers
laughing at my astonishment
Ah the jewel I'd found
locked inside my head

at six
it hung around my leg
every stumble
it followed
how I long to paint
find its shape
in the coloured shadows
behind the blackboard
fruits of wild imaginings

school was such a disappointment
chalked up in a straightjacket
of A to Z
2 plus 2
the ball is red

at ten
I fitted neatly into its skin
in every lesson
lava spitting nostrils flaring
an invisible steam-head
in silent raging
piling up its hills
and back down again
between stark pages
along its higglety-pigglety fence
with flaking scales

D's for Dragons
the teacher said
just try again

at fourteen
we were reluctant lovers
a snake in the grass
kissing at the back of class
waltzing along its strange path
through the history books
past Maths and French
shooting from the lumbering
hills of German

all those reluctant arrows
that fell dead
and silent
into a hostile land
called English
I tried to scrape its scales
wash its stench from my breath

to be or not to be
that was the question then

at eighteen
its was my only rebel friend
it followed as I fled
my black and blue inked jail
all the bright expectations
that turned to red
a quick escape
down concrete streets
past all the jumbled words spelling
dead end
straight into a graveyard called
oblivion
it was here we laid our weary heads
on the ghostly shoulders
of the government

just fill this in
the woman said

NEXT

D's for Dragons
D's for Dragons
D's for Dragons
the teacher said

just try again
just try again

Tumbling fools

they break in front of windows
the froth spilt
from the three a.m. shift
blasting freedom and pocketing
pictures of the insane
incoherent night mumblings
ending in breakfast hangovers

yet foxes still inhabit the gardens

If statues could talk

she stood once upon a time
a crooked child
beneath his stony feet
a refugee from school
her tears washed clean
in veils
in veils of drizzling rain
in oceans of gray
silence
she read his name
traced each curve each golden vein

once within his sheltering shadow
she spoke to him
spoke a myriad
of childish things
her longings
a thousand daisy-chains
her secret wish
to knit the future with the past
to sit it quietly upon her lap

and talk with him

walk with him

now she an old woman stands
bent withered and wrinkle-folded
stone-dusted flesh

years of wisdom
in a palm
snatching the beauty of moments
in the struggle of toil
or the loving glance
of this small boy
who questions now
did you know him?

and still, still he stands
frozen stone
his footprints moving
invisibly
through each day
each year
his granite stare
set along the distant horizon
his echo etched
forever here

Train

it departs
rumbling like a cat
each rivet
a rhythmic blast
from the roaring heart
a beast that stalks its prey
knows its way
through all the crooked
secret
backstreets alleys
highways
slipping past
a shuttered landscape
where mirrored windows wink
and sleepy sleepers wake

it escapes
freed from its tangled city strings
following its gray scented trail
through shadowed trees
and quiet hills
to a distant destination

destination
destination destination
destination destination destination
destination
as yet
unnamed

The granny I never had

silently she sits
posing herself
into a certain frame
that honest way
caught in time
her beauty
broken
broken so easily
slipping
rose-cheeked and fading
behind the floral arrangement
her fate
frozen in a smile

faded now, faded
she remains
where the dust settles
on ghost-petalled flowers
one solitary picture
cradled in a snapshot
wishful thoughts
a curious child
caught between the pages
of time's distant hands

Sylvia's mirror

did you see it flicker
that light
the eye
up close and personal
was it a lie
a 'terrible fish' that rises
chanting from its boggy crown
that thick black and shadowed worm
a terrorist in doubt

or was it a glimmer
something well known
washed from grit
rubbed and grown
cut from a cold cloth
quicksilver-edged
that 'four-cornered' god
calculating
its cruel and truthful eye still blinking
a sharp light
beneath the lake

Johnny's black cat

Johnny stared at the black cat
cracked open
with fascination
his sharp stick
prodding
probing
between its ribs
the gap within
mouth wide open in lifeless grin
eyes turned to vacant
oblivion

there Johnny stood
a roadside gazer
there he lingered
hooked
transfixed
flies buzzing in erotic bliss
by this casual grave
side-by-side
between life and decay
the great death lay...
empty?

Fish-wishing

fish-wishing
fish-wishing

I looked for you
in all the hustle
the bustle
caught within its struggle
a sticky embrace
entangled and engraved
in slate gray
day to day
searching to find a face
a look a smile
I a wish-fulfilling child
held in wait

I looked for you
in all the quiet places
under shadow-lit bowers
in broken summer showers
as the rain drops drip
from my brow to my lips
that sweet taste
the promise of your kiss
that's still to come

I looked for you
in all the hidden
through my deep forbidden

web-spun and spinning
in trumpets of autumn crimson
till its last heat
that beat
had fallen lost
beneath
beneath my weary feet

fish-wishing
fish-wishing

I think of you
I think of you

and thirst to fish
in all our sunny pools

these words
our bait
our line
our rod
our spool

fish-wishing
fish-wishing

I'll wait for you
I'll wait for you

Jonah's tree

I think of you
resting in the thick balcony of its shade
each bloom of thought
falling as fruit
another sentence for your page
another thought to contemplate
the world
and all man's silly ways
as he slips and stumbles on the road
a journey long and sometimes bitter cold
where truth and life are often cheaply sold

I dream of you
feet moored between its roots
your love a-sail twisting free to the wind
in the strong curve of its boughs
a body safe from harm
sheltering in its arms
those seeded regrets forgot
your heart now firmly planted
in seas of summer plenty
sitting at peace
at peace
beneath its dappled blanket

I sing to you
a leviathan's tune upon my lips
in the shadow of the stars
tongue-tied and lost in my watery bower

Puck's potion caught permanent in my eyes
a mermaid at a loss to know the words
that binding spell
to cross the slumber of time
so I might sit with you a man
who was swallowed by a whale
and found redemption

One night stand

blinking through the pluming smoke
a vacant space
beside the wall
candle-lit
the shifting shadows
slip
the corner of my eye
expectant breaths
of lost arrivals
inhale the invisible
an air
of ghostly corpses

I lay awake
restless and tossing
this purple light
emptying its burden
as shadows
rush to darkened corners
vibrations
distant voices
the muted calls of voiceless children
ringing in my ear

as a cigarette
still and burning
crumbles into ashes
the slow wick
of my despair

Shattered

it shattered when you left

and as I pushed it from its high cliff edge
I hoped you'd find that breath
those wings
leave all your fluttering fears
those ghostly chains
find at last
this your loving jailor
could not hold those cold
stifling woes and pains

it shattered when you left

and as it hit the stony floor
a thousand thoughts were left unsaid
split across its glassy edge
and all our wounded ways
those countless strains
that tumbled and rushed in frantic ways
spilt a dark stain
marked in red
as it fell to dusty death

it shattered when you left

in all the dusty longings
I tried to find myself again
glue its fragments back

but all the tiny cracks
the gaps
the broken words
the shards of your discontent
the glassy cuts and wounds
confound me
surround me
remind me
that although it broke years ago

it shattered when you left

She stood tall

true to the bone of her words
seed scattered and planted each sentence
each thought expressed
with the true cut of her jib
a stargazing Amazon
native still
beneath the skin
naked and unashamed
to paint with shade and dark
ready to love and fight
meet like with like

O how sweet and rare the wild flowers grow
in those lingering echoes and the beauty of her light

Doors

to sigh the last
in unexpected hope
and leap with curiosity
to what lies beyond the door

but souls cling to the body
their velvet cloaks
a journey's comfort
lingering in an ill-fitted masquerade

The end

there are no conclusions here
no illusions
no line is drawn
no stamp
to place this thought
neat into its little box
next to the one I had before lunch

there are no absolutions
no rights
no wrongs
no looks of disapproval
to echo through my head
to repeat
repeat
repeat again

there is no nothing
but the silence
these few words
when at last they reach
the end

Some other books published by **Luath Press**

Bad Ass Raindrop
Kokumo Rocks
1 84282 018 4 PB £6.99

What would happen if a raindrop took acid? Does your bum shake and does your belly wobble? And have you noticed that there are no black babies on 'New Baby' cards?

Fadeke Kokumo Rocks' poetry is alive with love, passion, humour and brutal honesty. It is sharply observed, potent and insightful, capturing beautifully the sixth dimension of the creative eye. It has a rich diversity of time and content which embraces the globe and its conflicts, domestic and urban.

You can hear the monsoon rains of Africa, taste the mangoes of India, touch the compassion and spirit of the child and sense the pain of burning flesh as race riots rage.

Read the eclectic, electrifying poetry of Kokumo Rocks in this collection containing over forty of her most popular poems. Full of Kokumo's distinctive humour, *Bad Ass Raindrop* challenges the questions we answer unquestioning.

Kokumo has been performing her poetry for the last ten years, and now, in her first published collection, she brings together her best work. Equally entertaining read or performed, Kokumo's distinctive voice and unique brand of humour shine through.

The Tiger Woods of performance poetry. ANGUS CALDER

Sex, Death and Football
Alistair Findlay
1 84282 022 2 PB £6.99

Football has never been a science so much as a heartbeat away from a sclaf, an unlucky bobble, catastrophe – a bit like Sex and Death – and thus a suitable case for poetry.
Alistair Findlay

Alistair Findlay takes a measured look at those three most important facets of life – sex, death, and of course football.

Showing great individuality, energy and wit, Findlay creates 'elegies – with edge' in this accessible and uncompromising collection. With his ear for natural human expression and appetite for life, he succeeds in crafting poetry teeming with both humanity and humour. His poems bridge the gap between perceptions of 'high' and popular culture, and tackle with rare insight the breadth of human experience, both sacred and profane.

An outstanding writer. If poetry remains meaningful to more than an elite few in the 21st century, it will be because of works such as this.
ROBERT ALAN JAMIESON

I like the energy and brio... the voice is strong and different and works well.
JACKIE KAY

Voyage of Intent
James Robertson
1 905222 26 2 PB £6.99

Poems and building match each other in a dialogue that takes in symbolism and geography, history, form and aspiration.

From an initially sceptical standpoint James Robertson, the first writer in residence in the Scottish Parliament, soon found that he admired the building of 'upturned boats' and the enthusiasm of those who sail her.

Here are eleven sonnets and three essays written from his time spent in the building. They create snapshots of the building and the people working and living in and around it, and convey the historical relationship between Scottish literature, identity, politics and the Royal Mile as a literary location.

For in the end a Parliament is not a building, but a voyage of intent, a journey to whatever we might be.

...piercing analysis of what is left of Scotland's literary heritage.
THE HERALD

Tartan & Turban

Bashabi Fraser

1 84282 044 3 PB £8.99

'Read Bashabi Fraser's poetry and experience a swirl of emotions and images.'

A Bengali poet living in Scotland, Bashabi Fraser creatively spans the different worlds she inhabits, celebrating the contrasts of the two countries whilst also finding commonality. Focusing on clear themes and issues – displacement, removal, belonging, identity, war – her poetry is vibrant with feeling and comes alive in an outrageous game of sound patterns.

Bashabi's lyrical and evocative verses... touch a chord with all those who hear her. THE SUNDAY STATESMAN, CALCUTTA

Two cultures, two worlds and a writer who can span them both.
VALERIE BIERMAN

Burning Whins

Liz Niven

1 84282 074 5 PB £8.99

Burning Whins *concerns itself with relationships and ownership.*

Describing the Scottish Parliament, plane travel in the Western Isles, and the destruction wrought by the recent Foot and Mouth epidemic with equal familiarity and fluidity, these poems depict the many faces of contemporary Scotland with grace and intimacy.

Liz Niven is also a poet whose works in Scots give real presence and immediacy to this dynamic and descriptive language. *Burning Whins* cements Liz's presence as a contributor to the development of modern Scots and its linguistic place in the nation's cultural growth patterns.

Her words fall softly like music into the open shell of the eager listener's ear.
JEREMY HODGES, DAILY MAIL